Computer Neural Networks

On MATLAB

Daniel Okoh

Foreword

The book 'Computer neural networks on MATLAB' is a complete package on how to engage the neural network toolbox of MATLAB to predict any variable that is expressible in time series format. The book is written with an approach that is easy to understand. It is a product of sound commitment and deep desire to share knowledge with wider community.

The author of the book, Daniel Okoh, is a brilliant early career scientist with passion for multidisciplinary intelligent research. With first class bachelor degree in Physics, a PhD from a leading Nigerian institution, and a couple of experience at a number of leading international scientific laboratories, including an overseas graduate training; Okoh has indeed been endowed with great potential which is demonstrated in this classic, 'Computer neural networks on MATLAB'. He is a regular resource person at MATLAB training schools at local and international levels.

The book is a must have training manual for anyone with interest in application of neural networks to any form of time series process. In five chapters, and with illustrated examples, the book clearly explained how to apply computer neural networks on MATLAB in modeling and forecasting any time series variable. Books that reveal all secrets of detailed programming like this are quite rare. It is with great pleasure and deep sense of trust that I recommend the book to every serious researcher at all levels. With this book on Computer neural networks on MATLAB', speaking MATLAB becomes a fun!

Professor Babatunde Rabiu
Director/Chief Executive, Centre for Atmospheric Research,
National Space Research & Development Agency,
Anyigba, Nigeria

Preface

Computer neural networks are a branch of artificial intelligence, inspired to behave in a manner similar to the human brain; they are trained and they learn from their training. Computer neural networks have a wide variety of applications, mostly hinged around modeling, forecasting, and general predictions.

This book illustrates how to use computer neural networks on MATLAB in very simple and elegant manner. The language of the book is elementary as it is meant for beginners; readers are not assumed to have previous skills on the subject. Projects, in varying degrees, have been used to make sure that readers get a practical and hands-on experience on the subject. The book is meant for you if you want to get a quick start with the practical use of computer neural networks on MATLAB without the boredom associated with a lengthy theoretical write-up.

Table of Contents

Chapter 1

General Introduction to Computer Neural Networks

In this book, our interest is to present how neural networks are used in the MATLAB software, but before we do so, we first present a brief introduction which we think is necessary especially for beginners.

Computer neural networks (also called 'artificial neural networks' or just 'neural networks' for short) belong to a branch of artificial intelligence called machine learning. They are a system of information processing techniques inspired by the manner in which the human brain works, and so the name 'neural network'.

Neural networks can 'learn' trends and patterns in data and consequently be able to correctly predict future trends and data patterns. They are therefore hugely applied in predictive modeling where they are used to make predictions of how events (like temperature, population, stock market, etc.) will occur in the future. Neural networks are also applied in character recognition (e.g. to recognize handwritten characters).

They have been used in the financial industry for economic indicator forecasts, price forecasts, fraud detection, credit worthiness, etc. They have also been used in the field of medicine for detection and evaluation of medical phenomena, treatment cost estimation, medical diagnosis, etc. In manufacturing industries, neural networks have been used for quality and process controls. Scientists have used them for pattern recognition, gene recognition, physical system modeling, etc. There are actually an inexhaustible number of applications for neural networks.

The strengths and advantages of neural networks are in their ability to represent both linear and non-linear relationships directly from the data being modeled. Traditional linear models are simply inadequate when it comes to true modeling of data that contains non-linear characteristics (Baboo and Shereef, 2010).

Neural networks are basically structured in 3 layers: an input layer, a hidden layer, and an output layer. As the names imply, the input and output layers respectively contain data passed into the system and information gotten out of it. We'll explain this well when we take practical examples in subsequent chapters. The hidden layer contains the processes between the input and the output layers. This is where the real processing of the input data into the output information is done, and it is so called because the processes are supposedly 'hidden' from users.

Each layer may contain one or more units (that are also called neurons). For example, we can have 4 neurons in the input layer, 7 neurons in the hidden layer, and 1 neuron in the output layer. Then the architecture of the neural network is said to be 4-7-1. If the architecture of a neural network is 6-19-2, it therefore means that the network has 6 input layer neurons, 19 hidden layer neurons, and 2 output layer neurons. Figure 1 is an illustration of a neural network with architecture 3-5-1. Neurons on one layer are connected to those on the next layer using connections (also called 'weights') as shown in Figure 1.

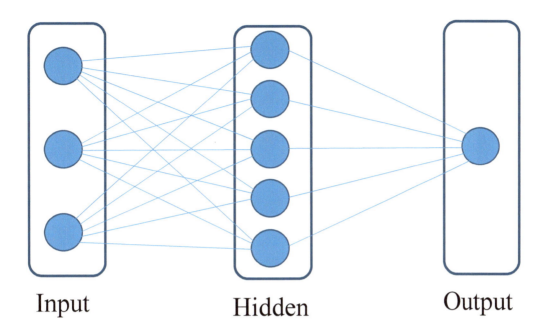

Figure 1. Schematic Illustration of a Neural Network with Architecture 3-5-1

The number of input and output layer neurons can usually be decided from the system of problem to be solved, but this is not the case with the number of hidden layer neurons. The above statement will be well understood when we treat practical projects as in the next chapters, but for now, we vaguely state that the number of hidden layer neurons are arbitrarily decided. We will understand this shortly.

Chapter 2

The Neural Network Fitting Tool on MATLAB

For a first time user of neural network on the MATLAB software, we recommend the MATLAB neural network fitting tool (called the 'nftool'). The tool is a very elegant one for training neural networks, it is also simple and straightforward to use. Without wasting further time, we pick a project and illustrate how to do the project using the nftool.

2.1 Project 1: Time Series Modeling of Daily Maximum Surface Temperatures

For this project, we have placed most of the resources that will be required at the MATLAB Central website (http://www.mathworks.com/matlabcentral/fileexchange/59362-neural-network-training-code). To follow the step-by-step guide on this book, we recommend for the reader to download the compressed file on this website. The compressed file contains a folder named "MATLAB NN" and everything we will need is contained in this folder. We shall from now on refer to this folder as our Project Folder.

Our aim in this project is to illustrate how neural networks can be used to model daily maximum surface temperatures at any location on Earth. For the case of this project, we will use data obtained for a station in Eudunda, South Australia (Latitude 34.18°S, Longitude 139.08°E, and Elevation 415m). The data was obtained from the climatic online data website of the Australian Bureau of Meteorology (http://www.bom.gov.au/climate/data/).

First, we extracted the required data and arranged them in 3 columns: the 1st column represents the Year, the 2nd column represents the Day of Year, and the 3rd column represents the maximum surface temperature observed for the day. This data is stored in the file named 'Eudunda1.txt' on our Project Folder. Figure 2 is a representation of a portion of the data in this file. The data file 'Eudunda1.txt' contains available data from the website covering the period from years 1965 to 2015.

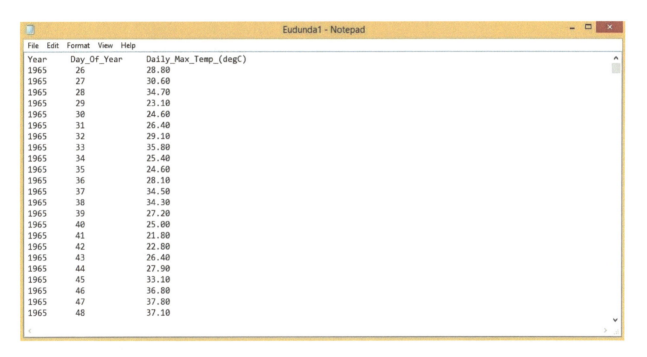

Figure 2. Sample of Daily Maximum Surface Temperature Data

The first 2 columns (Year, and Day of Year) are time series indicators for the data, while the 3rd column is the data itself. In our neural network setting, we will regard the first 2 columns as the input dataset, and the 3rd column as the target dataset. By extension, the target dataset corresponds to the output dataset when the neural network is used to make the prediction. So, if we were to train a network using the above data, we will automatically have 2 input layer neurons (Year, and Day of Year) and 1 output layer neuron (the daily maximum surface temperature). As explained earlier in chapter 1, we won't be able to precisely decide the best suitable number of hidden layer neurons yet, until we begin the training.

Now, let's begin!

2.2 The Neural Network Training

1. The first step is to launch the neural network fitting tool. To do this, simply type the word *nftool* on the MATLAB command window, and hit the Enter button. A window similar to what we have in Figure 3 should appear.

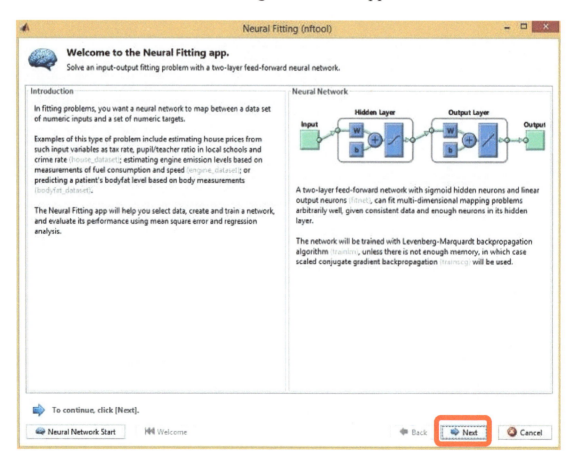

Figure 3. Interface of the MATLAB's Neural Network Fitting Tool.

The window basically contains a brief introduction to Neural Networks, especially as implemented on the nftool. You are not expected to do anything here! Just click the Next Button, and the window as shown in Figure 4 appears.

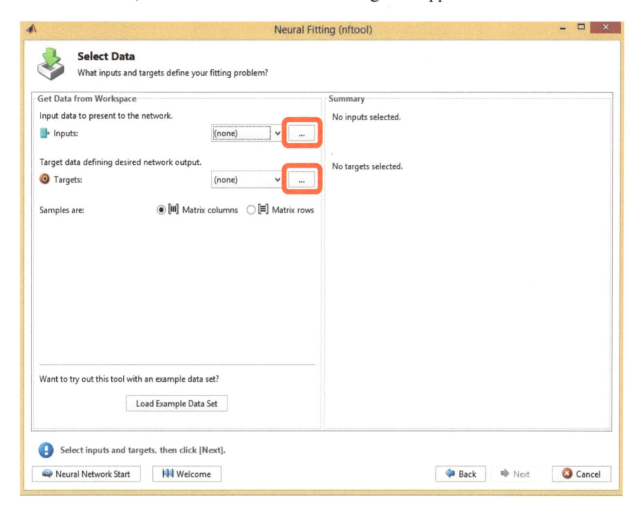

Figure 4. Loading the Input and Target Data.

2. Now, use the browse buttons highlighted (in red color)in Figure 4 to import the input and the target data. Recall the input data are in columns 1 and 2 of the data in Eudunda1.txt, while the target data are in column 3 of the same file. For the sake of simplicity, we have split the data appropriately into 2 files to contain the input and

the target data as shown in Figure 5. We have also included these 2 files in our Project Folder; they are respectively named Inputs1.txt and Targets1.txt.

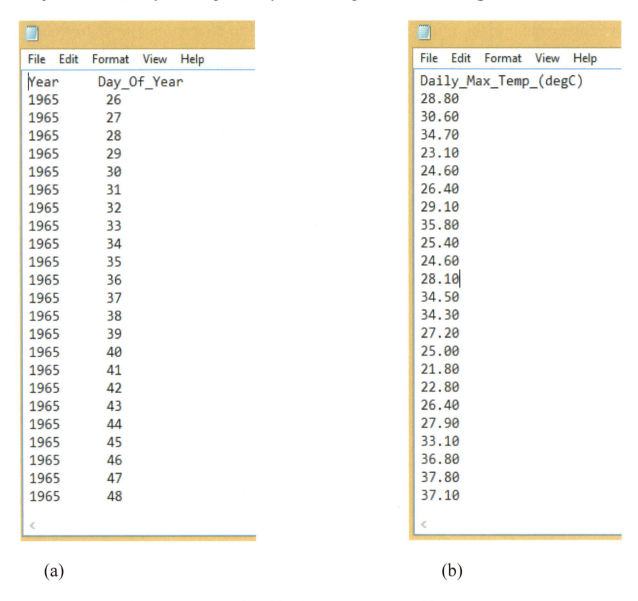

(a)   (b)

Figure 5. (a) The Input Data File (b) The Target Data File

Clicking the Inputs browse button allows us to browse to the location of the input file on our computer (see Figure 6).

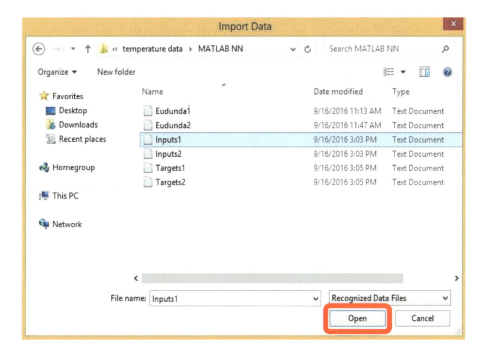

Figure 6. Selecting the Input Data.

Select the input data file and click the Open button to import the data. The next window is the import wizard (shown in Figure 7).

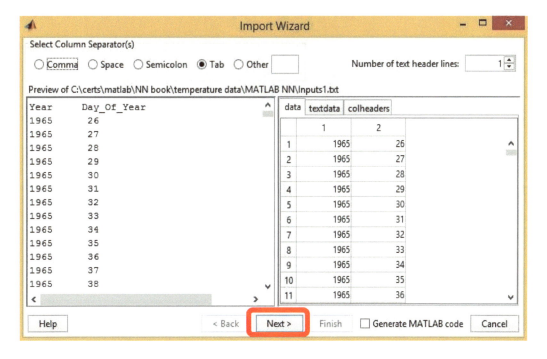

Figure 7. The Import Wizard Step 1.

Click the Next button to proceed to the next step on the import wizard.

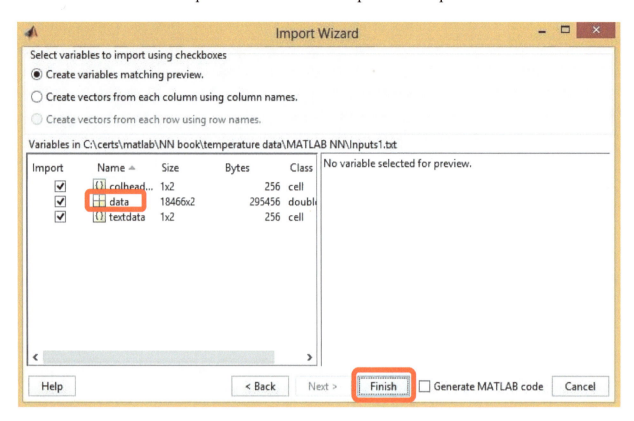

Figure 8. The Import Wizard Step 2.

We can rename the variable named data (highlighted in red color) just to distinguish it from the similar variable we'll get when we import the target data. Click on the Finish button to exit the import wizard and return to the nftool window. At this stage, we have imported the input dataset into the neural network fitting too. You should repeat a very similar procedure to import the target dataset, and when you are done, the nftool window looks as shown in Figure 9, with indications of the sizes of the imported data on the Summary pane of the window.

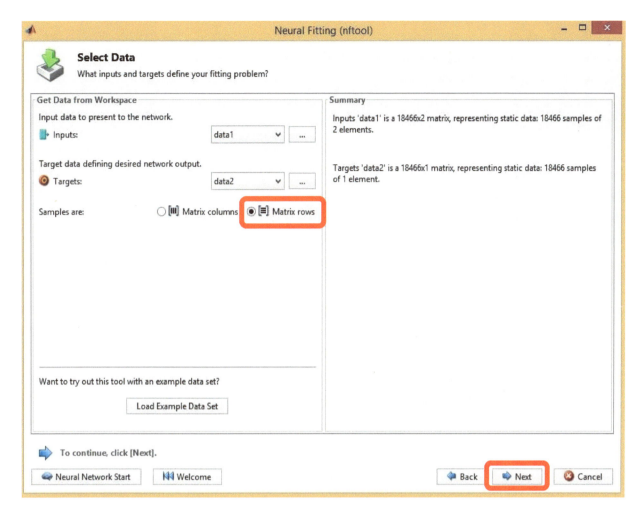

Figure 9. The nftool after importing the Input and the Target Data.

The Summary pane shows that we have imported input data with 18,466 samples of 2 elements, and target data with 18,466 samples of 1 element. Remember to tick that Samples are Matrix rows!

It is important and necessary to check that the number of samples in the input data is the same as in the target data. Then click the Next button to continue.

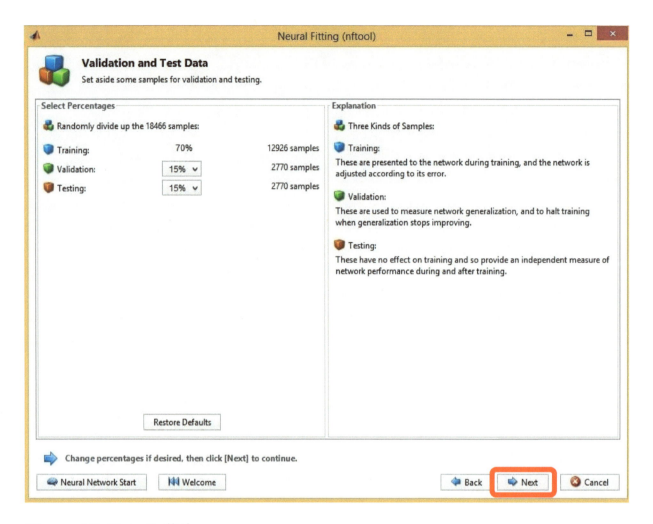

Figure 10. Data Splitting.

3. The next stage is to split the data. It is usually the practice to split data for a comprehensive neural network training into the following 3 sets; the training set, the validation set, and the testing set. The training set is used for the 'actual' training, the validation set is used to ensure that the network attains a desired performance in generalization, and the testing set is used to test the performance of the network after validation.

As can be seen in Figure 10, there is a frequently used standard where 70% of the data is used for the actual training, 15% for validating, and the remaining 15% for testing. This is the default setting for the nftool, but users can always share the data in their desired proportions. The splitting is also done randomly, so that bias is not intentionally introduced into the system.

If this is OK, then hit the Next button to get the next window as shown in Figure 11.

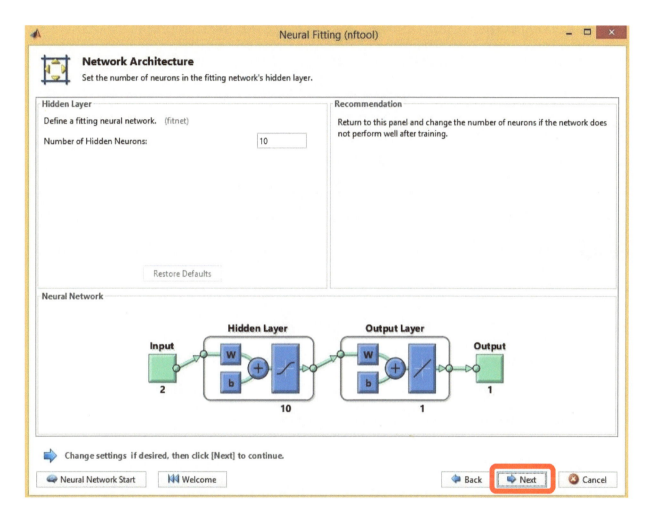

Figure 11. Entering the Number of Hidden Layer Neuron.

4. Enter the number of hidden layer neurons. This is one very crucial aspect of training a neural network. As we have previously mentioned, the number of input and output layer neurons can be decided from the system of problem to be solved,

but the number of hidden layer neurons cannot. For example, we have already observed in this project that the number of input layer neurons is 2 (the Year, and the Day of Year) and that the number of output layer neuron is 1 (the daily maximum surface temperature). We, however, have not known an appropriate value for the number of hidden layer neurons.

There are no specific or perfect rules for deciding the most appropriate number of neurons in a hidden layer. Using an excessive number of hidden-layer neurons will result in over-fitting, while using a fewer number will result in under-fitting. Either scenario usually degrades the generalization capability of the network. This is specifically the problem; using a fewer number means that the network will not be able to learn enough that will make it give good predictions, while using an excessive number means that it will be able to learn so much of the data used for the training that it will not be able to give good predictions for data that is outside of the set used for the training.

There is a method that is reliable and frequently used, but at this stage, we will not want to bore readers with those intricacies. We will explain the method in the next chapter of this book. For now, we want the reader to be able to progress successfully to the end of training a network that is just good.

As can be seen in Figure 11, the nftool (by default) suggests a value 10 for the number of hidden layer neurons. We may change this value to a different value, but at this stage, we suggest it's OK to progress with it that way. So just click the next button to get the next window as illustrated in Figure 12.

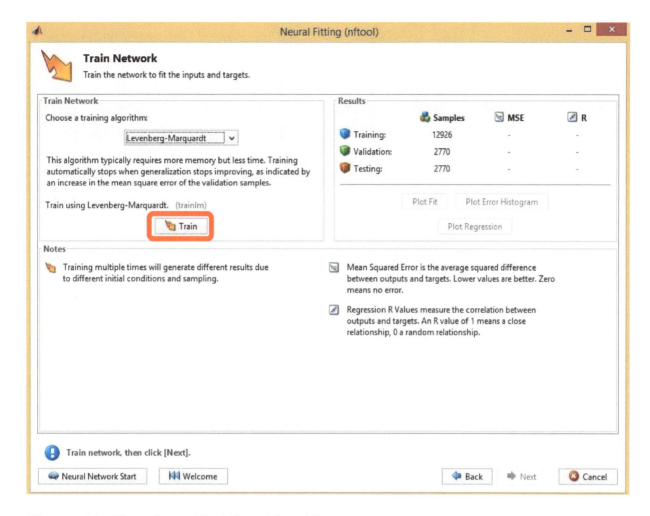

Figure 12. Choosing a Training Algorithm.

5. The next stage is to choose a training algorithm. Neural network trainings proceed in different patterns as described in different algorithms. There are quite a number of neural network algorithm, but for a first timer who doesn't know what to expect, we recommend the Levenberg-Marquardt algorithm which is also default on the nftool.

The Levenberg-Marquardt algorithm (detailed in Levenberg (1944)) is highly admired and used because of its speed and efficiency in learning (Demuth and Beale, 2002; Kisi and Uncuoglu, 2005; Okoh et al., 2016). The algorithm requires more computer memory but takes less time. These days, almost all of our computers have more than the required memory, and so this is usually not a problem.

Click the Train button, and the training begins in a new window as shown in Figure 13.

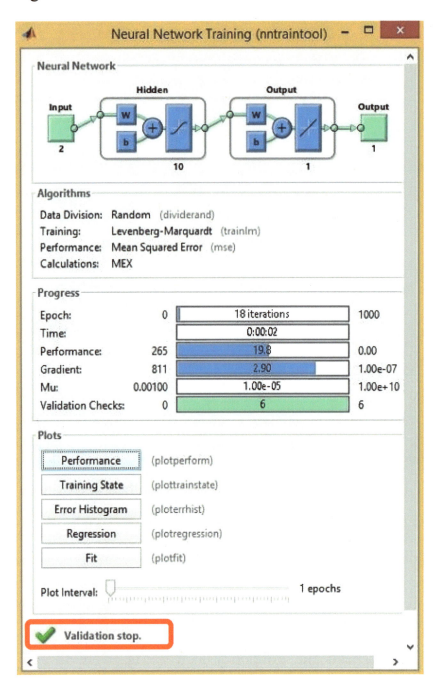

Figure 13. Training the Network.

Congratulations once you see the Validation stop sign as highlighted in Figure 13. You have successfully trained a neural network. There are a number of things on this window that are worth understanding as one progresses in expertise of neural network training, but since we don't want to bore you with them at this stage, you may close the window to return to the nftool window as shown in Figure 14.

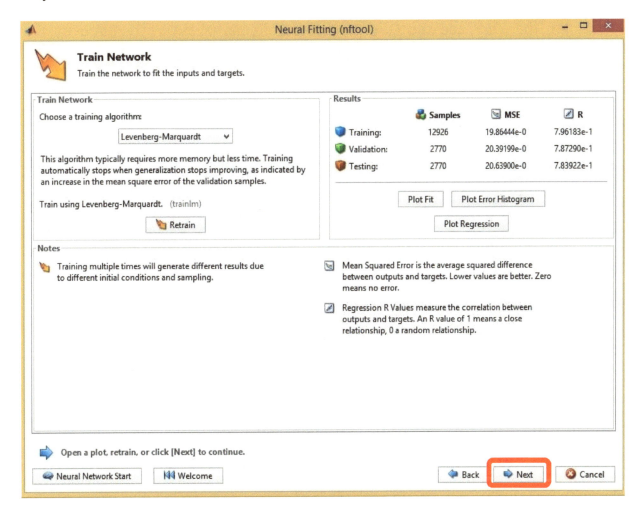

Figure 14. Results of the Neural Network Training.

The Result pane on Figure 14 shows results of the neural network training in terms of the mean-squared errors (MSE) and the correlation coefficients (R). It is at this stage that we wish to reveal some of the things that go on inside the nftool so as to also be able to elegantly explain the results.

Ultimately, at the end of this training, a network was created. In the next few sections that follow, we will explain how to save and use this network. This network is the most important item we need to pick from the training.

It is this network that we will be needing to make predictions. For this project, it is the one that will tell us the daily maximum temperatures for a day in any year we desire. So, the Year and the Day of year are inputs (they are required by the network to make predictions) while the daily maximum temperature is the output (it is to be predicted by the network). Recall that measured values of daily maximum temperatures are called targets.

In summary, the targets are the 'true' measurements (that is, the temperature data that we started with) while the outputs are the predictions which the network will make.

When the network makes a prediction, we can compare this prediction with the true measurement if is available. For instance, we know from the data used for the training that the maximum temperature for the 26th day of 1965 is 28.8°C (see the first data line in Figure 2). We can now request the network to predict the maximum temperature for this same day (how to do this will be practically illustrated in the next section of this chapter), and it for instance predicts 29.3°C. There is a 0.5°C difference between the prediction (also called the output) and the observation (also called the target). This difference is called the error of the prediction. If the error is small, then the network prediction is good, but if the error is large, then the network prediction is bad. So, the best networks always give the least errors.

One set of results we see on the Result pane of Figure 14is the Mean of Squared Errors (MSE). There is an MSE for the training, for the validation, and for the testing datasets. This is how the MSE is computed: Given any dataset, let's say the testing dataset (which in this project is a total of 2770 samples), it contains the inputs and the targets (T). We first use the network to make the predictions (P) for each of the 2770 days. When these predictions are subtracted from corresponding targets, we get the errors (E=T-P). When we square each of the errors and take their mean, we get the MSE which is mathematically described in equation 1.

$$MSE = \frac{\sum_{i=1}^{N}(T_i - P_i)^2}{N} \tag{1}$$

where N is the total number of samples which is 2770 for the testing dataset. The root of the MSE is another usually preferred measure of the error. It is called the root-mean-squared error (RMSE) and described mathematically in equation 2. The RMSE is preferred to the MSE because it has the same unit as the quantity involved (temperature in this case), and so makes it easy to fathom how close the network predictions are to the observations. The MSE is in square units of the quantity.

$$RMSE = \sqrt{\frac{\sum_{i=1}^{N}(T_i - P_i)^2}{N}} \tag{2}$$

Figure 14 shows that the MSEs for the network obtained in this project are approximately 19.86, 20.39, and 20.64 for the training, validating, and testing datasets respectively. Taking the roots, we get the RMSEs as 4.46, 4.52, and 4.54. It means that there are errors of about 4.5°C on the datasets.

Another set of results we see on the Result pane of Figure 14 is regression (R). It is an indication of how the predictions are related to the observations. Values of R close to 1 means there is good correlation between the predictions and the observations. Values close to 0 mean that the correlation between them is bad. In neural network trainings, we use the regression values to understand if we may accept the produced network or not. Figure 14 shows that the R values in our project are approximately 0.80, 0.79, and 0.78 for the training, validation, and testing datasets respectively. The values are quite close to 1, so we may accept the network.

Click the Next button to continue to the next window as illustrated in Figure 15.

2.3 Optional Additional Testing

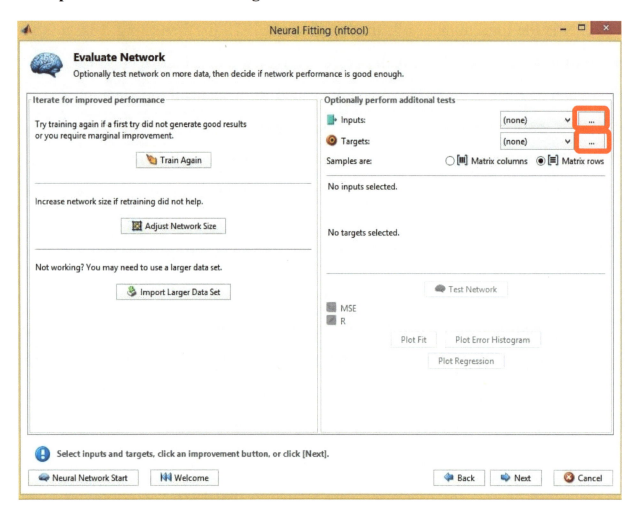

Figure 15. Optional Additional Testing, Step 1.

Here, we can optionally perform another test if we have another dataset we planned to use. This is usually necessary if there is particular dataset we want to test the network with. This step is not necessary but can be used to satisfy our curiosity as to the performance of the network on our own choice of test dataset [Remember that the testing dataset earlier used is a random 15% of the data we supplied, so we not exactly sure of what constituted that dataset].

In this project, we have intentionally set aside data for year 2016 so that we can use them for additional testing. Here, our intention is to understand if the network also performs well in forecasting (that is in predicting future values). This data is also contained in our project folder; the data files are named as Inputs2.txt and Targets2.txt respectively for the input and target data.

As we did before, we use the Input and the Target browse buttons to import the input and target data respectively. After doing these, we get the window as shown in Figure 16.

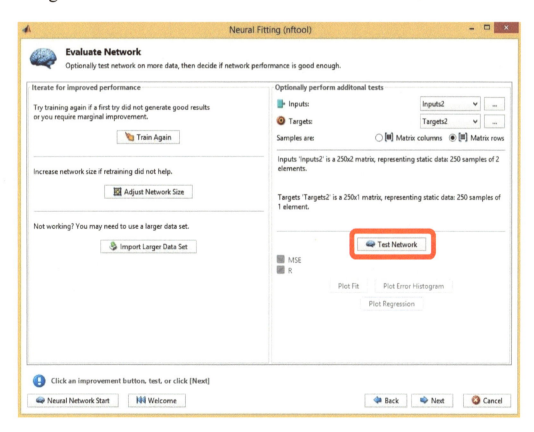

Figure 16. Optional Additional Testing, Step 2.

Now click the Test Network button to see the results as shown in Figure 17.

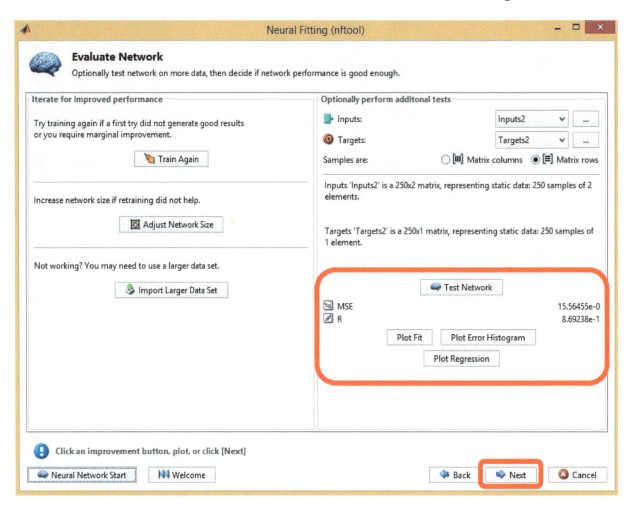

Figure 17. Test results for additional testing.

The results show that the MSE is 15.56 (that means RMSE is 3.94), and that the regression value is 0.87. Interestingly the network gave a lower RMSE for this dataset compared to the RMSE we got earlier with the training dataset. This further increases the confidence level for the network. And like we said earlier, this additional testing is completely optional.

Now, click the Next button to proceed to the next window as illustrated in Figure 18.

2.4 Saving the Network

Here, we are interested in getting the network and its properties out in a reusable form. This is what we will be needing to make the network prediction for any given day.

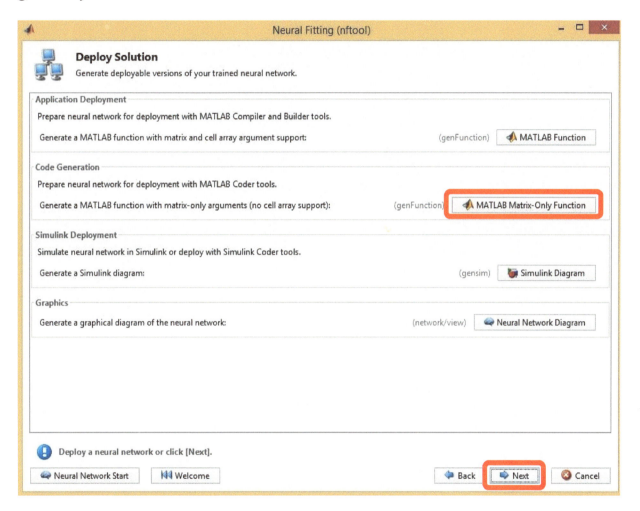

Figure 18. Saving the Network 1.

The four push buttons on the right hand side of Figure 18 can be used to obtain various information/properties of the network, but to keep things straight, we will concentrate on the 'MATLAB Matrix-Only Function' which is highlighted as shown in Figure 18. Clicking on this button enables us to save a MATLAB function which we can later use to make the network predictions. Precisely, the button generates a MATLAB code containing the properties/parameters of the network and the equations that transform the inputs into outputs. Without hesitation, let's see what this looks like.

Click the 'MATLAB Matrix-Only Function' button. This will generate a MATLAB code as illustrated in Figure 19. The code is a MATLAB function, and in this case, the name of the function is 'myNeuralNetworkFunction' as can be seen on line 1 of the code. Save the code with this same name, and return to the nftool window as in Figure 18.

```
1   function [y1] = myNeuralNetworkFunction(x1)
2   %MYNEURALNETWORKFUNCTION neural network simulation function.
3   %
4   % Generated by Neural Network Toolbox function genFunction, 19-Sep-2016 1
5   %
6   % [y1] = myNeuralNetworkFunction(x1) takes these arguments:
7   %   x = Qx2 matrix, input #1
8   % and returns:
9   %   y = Qx1 matrix, output #1
10  % where Q is the number of samples.
11
12  %#ok<*RPMT0>
13
14  % ===== NEURAL NETWORK CONSTANTS =====
```

Figure 19. MATLAB Function Describing the Network Generated.

In the next section, we will describe how to use this code to make predictions. At this stage, the network code has been saved.

Finally, on the nftool window, click the Next button to continue to the last window as shown in Figure 20.

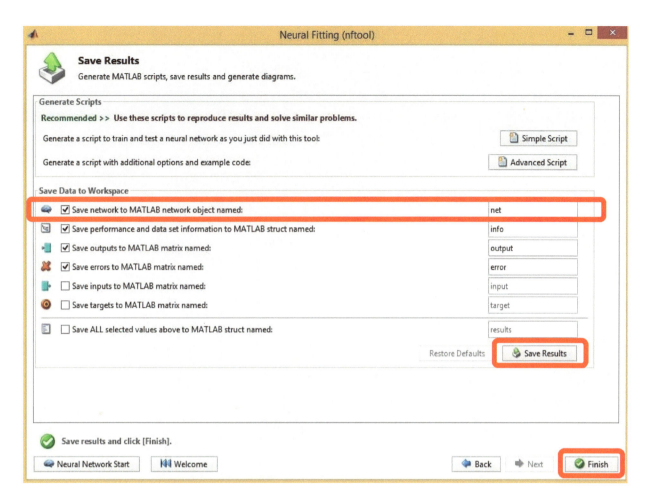

Figure 20. Saving the Network 2.

This window allows us to save results of the network. Most importantly for us at this stage is to be able to save the network itself. This is the first item on the list of items to save in Figure 20. It has been checked by default, and so we just click on the 'Save Results' button to save it. The default name for the network is *net*, we may change the name but this is not necessary.

We can now exit the nftool window by clicking the Finish button.

Note that the network we just saved is actually saved in MATLAB's workspace as illustrated in Figure 21(a). This saving is temporal because the network will be lost when we close the MATLAB software.

To save the network permanently on your computer, right-click on it, and then click the *Save As...* button as illustrated in Figure 21(b).

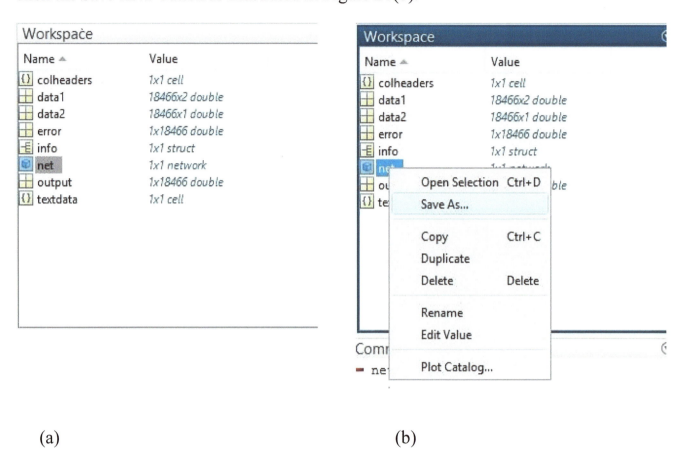

(a)   (b)

Figure 21. The Network saved on the Workspace

At this stage, we have both the network and a code describing its mathematical formulation saved permanently on our computer. The next stage is to be able to use either of them to make predictions.

2.5 Making Neural Network Predictions from the Saved Code

As explained earlier, the saved code is a MATLAB function. The command required to run it is: *myNeuralNetworkFunction(x1)* where*myNeuralNetworkFunction* is the name of the function as well as the name of the saved file, and *x1* is the input data for which the prediction is required. If, for instance, we want the network to predict the maximum temperature for day 313 of year 2018, then the input will be x1=[2018 313]. Then when we run the command: *myNeuralNetworkFunction(x1)*, it gives us the maximum temperature for the day.

For this project, we have saved the network code in the project folder with the name *myNeuralNetworkFunction.m*. To run it, simply change the MATLAB Current Folder location to the project folder or to wherever location you saved the code on your computer (This is in case you already hadn't done so). Then enter and run the codes:

```
x1=[2018 313]
myNeuralNetworkFunction(x1)
```

on your MATLAB command window or through the MATLAB editor. This should give 26.1126, which is the network's prediction of the maximum temperature for the 313th day of year 2018.

At one go, we can also predict the temperatures for as many days as we desire. Let's say we want the maximum temperature predictions for the 12th and 171st days in 2017, we also want the predictions for the 45th and 300th days of 2018, and also for the 9th and 276th days of year 2019, then only our inputs will change, the code to run is as illustrated below:

```
x1=[2017 12; 2017 171; 2018 45; 2018 300; 2019 9; 2019 276]
myNeuralNetworkFunction(x1)
```

This will give us the following 6 values as the respective maximum temperatures for those days: 31.8069, 13.4480, 30.3106, 24.8378, 32.0727, 21.5972.

And in case you already have the inputs saved in a file like *Inputs2.txt* on our project folder, then you can simply get the data into MATLAB as x1, and then run *myNeuralNetworkFunction(x1)*.In the code that follows below, we have used the dlmread function to read the data from Inputs2.txt, and after running the myNeuralNetworkFunction function, we used the dlmwrite function to write the outputs to a file named Outputs2.txt [If you have any problem understanding lines 1 and 3 of the code, see our previous book on MATLAB Scripting and File Processing].

```
x1=dlmread('Inputs2.txt');
outputs=myNeuralNetworkFunction(x1);
fid=fopen('Outputs2.txt', 'wt'); fprintf(fid, '%f\n', outputs'); fclose(fid);
```

The data in Outputs2.txt are the network predictions for the inputs in Inputs2.txt (that is, days 1 to 258 of year 2016). The actual observations are saved in the file named Targets2.txt. Now, we can create a plot of the model predictions and the actual observations for days 1 to 258 of year 2016, so as to visualize how the predictions compare with the observations. The code required to do so is as follows, and the plot generated is as shown in Figure 22.

```
inputs=dlmread('Inputs2.txt');
targets=dlmread('Targets2.txt');
outputs=dlmread('Outputs2.txt');
doy=inputs(:,2);
plot(doy, targets); hold on; plot(doy, outputs, 'linewidth', 3);
legend('Targets', 'Outputs'); xlim([0 260]);
xlabel('Day of Year'); ylabel('Daily Maximum Temperature (^oC)');
```

Lines 1 to 3 of the code were used to read the input, target, and output data from the respective files where they are contained. The 4th line gives the name *doy* to the second column of the input data (This is the *day of year* column). These were treated in our previous book on MATLAB Scripting and File Processing. Lines 5 to 7 contain the codes for creating the plot in Figure 22. Details on how to create such plots are explained in another of our books on 2-D Line Graphs on MATLAB.

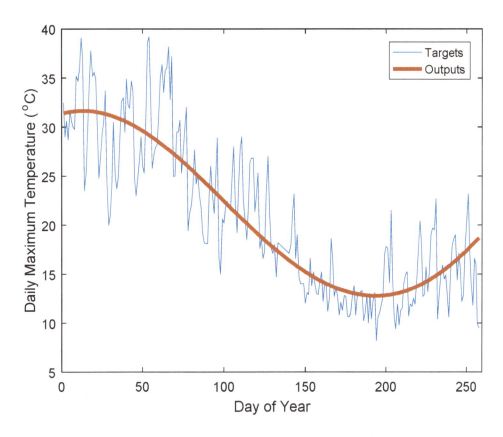

Figure 22. Plot of Neural Network Predictions and Actual Observations for year 2016 (Targets are the observations, while Outputs are the predictions).

Finally, we could also use MATLAB functions to construct our inputs especially if there is a sequence. For example, let's say we want to predict the maximum temperatures for all the days in year 2017. Then, our inputs as usual will be a matrix in 2 columns (the first column for the year and the second column for the day of year) and 365 rows (for the 365 days in the year). The first column contains the number 2017 repeated all through, while the second column contains integer numbers from 1 to 365. The commands required to generate this matrix are contained in lines 1 to 3 of the code below (It will be useful to read our book on Introduction to MATLAB if that part of the code is not very clear to you). Line 4 uses the *myNeuralNetworkFunction* to generate the network predictions for input data. Lines 5 and 6 create a plot of the predictions as shown in Figure 23.

```
inputs1=ones(365,1)*2017;    %column 1 of the input matrix
inputs2=(1:365)';    %column 2 of the input matrix
inputs=[inputs1 inputs2];   ;    %both columns of the input matrix put together
outputs=myNeuralNetworkFunction(inputs);  %network predictions for the inputs
plot(inputs2, outputs, 'linewidth', 3);  %plotting the network predictions
xlim([0 365]);ylim([5 40]);    %setting limits of the axes
xlabel('Day of Year'); ylabel('Daily Maximum Temperature (^oC)'); %axes labels
```

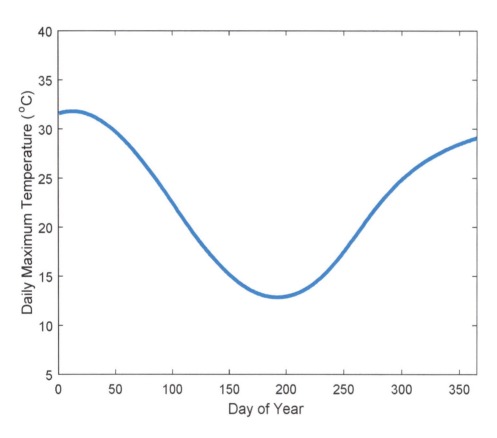

Figure 23. Plot of Neural Network Predictions for year 2017.

Actual observations were not included in the plot of Figure 23 because, at the time of writing this book, the observations have not been made. Figure 22 however clearly indicates that the network predictions are good fits of the observations.

2.6 Making Neural Network Predictions from the Saved Network

Here, the interest is the same as in the previous section except that we will now be doing so using the network itself, rather than the *myNeuralNetworkFunction* code. Most of the procedures are the same, except that here, we need to always load the network using the MATLAB load function. The command for doing this is: load net [where *net* is the name of the network, that is, the name we used to save the network]. After that, we then use the MATLAB sim function to simulate the network for any desired inputs. The command is: sim(net, inputs) [where *inputs* are the inputs we want to predict for].

For the sake of illustration, we have included the network created on this project to our project folder, it is named net10. The code below illustrates how can use the saved network to predict the maximum temperature for day 313 of year 2018 (like we previously did using the saved code.

```
input=[2018 313];    %input
load net10;    %load the network
output=sim(net, input');  %simulate the network for the input supplied
```

The single quotation mark used after the input in line 3 of the code is to transpose the input; the MATLAB network is usually constructed by default to regard samples as columns, but in this book, we have always regarded samples as rows. Running the above code gives us the output as 26.1126, which is the exact same result we got earlier using the saved code. Repeating the same predictions as we earlier did with the saved code, we should get the same results. Below are the commands we will need.

1. To predict the maximum temperatures for the 12th and 171st days in 2017, for the 45th and 300th days of 2018, and for the 9th and 276th days of year 2019:

```
inputs=[2017 12; 2017 171; 2018 45; 2018 300; 2019 9; 2019 276]; %inputs
load net10;    %load the network
outputs=sim(net, inputs'); %simulate the network for the inputs supplied
```

This also gives exactly same results as we got in the previous section. That is: 31.8069, 13.4480, 30.3106, 24.8378, 32.0727, 21.5972 respectively for those 6 days.

2. To predict the maximum temperatures for the days contained in the Inputs2.txt file, and to plot the outputs alongside the targets contained in the Targets2.txt file:

```
inputs=dlmread('Inputs2.txt');   %read the input data
targets=dlmread('Targets2.txt');%read the target data
doy=inputs(:,2);  %doy is column 2 of the input data
load net10;    %load the network
outputs=sim(net, inputs'); %simulate the network for the inputs supplied
plot(doy, targets); hold on; %plot the targets
plot(doy, outputs, 'linewidth', 3); %plot the outputs
legend('Targets', 'Outputs'); xlim([0 260]);
xlabel('Day of Year'); ylabel('Daily Maximum Temperature (^oC)');
```

The code produces exactly same plot as we have in Figure 22.

3. To predict and plot the maximum temperatures for all the days in year 2017:

```
inputs1=ones(365,1)*2017;    %column 1 of the input matrix
inputs2=(1:365)';   %column 2 of the input matrix
inputs=[inputs1 inputs2];  ;   %both columns of the input matrix put together
load net10;    %load the network
outputs=sim(net, inputs'); %simulate the network for the inputs supplied
plot(inputs2, outputs, 'linewidth', 3); %plotting the network predictions
xlim([0 365]); ylim([5 40]);   %setting limits of the axes
```

xlabel('Day of Year'); ylabel('Daily Maximum Temperature (^oC)'); %axes labels

This code also produces the exact same plot as we have in Figure 23.

So, we could either use the code or the network itself to make the neural network predictions.

Chapter 3

Deciding the Number of Neurons in the Hidden Layer

As earlier explained, there are no perfect rules for deciding the appropriate number of neurons in the hidden layer. There is however a reliable method which is most widely practiced. The method involves training different networks with different number of hidden layer neurons on the same dataset, and at the end of it all, choosing to use the network that gave the best performance (in the sense of giving the least errors).

Let's illustrate with the project in Chapter 2. We will need to repeat the entire procedure, but each time we do so, we should use a different number of hidden layer neurons (as in the stage of Figure 11). Then at the end of each training, we also make a record of the RMSE corresponding to the particular number of hidden layer neuron used. At the end of all trainings, we then use the particular network associated with the least RMSE.

If the test data we are using is randomly picked, there is a more likely tendency to obtain lower RMSEs by increasing the number of hidden layer neurons. This seems to suggest that if we want to get a better network (that is a network with smaller RMSE), we should use a higher value for the number of hidden layer neurons. There is need however to be careful not to over-train the network. If the network is over-trained, it will predict data within the years 1965 to 2015 very accurately (with smaller RMSEs), but for the 2016 data, the RMSEs will be higher.

To illustrate this, we have again trained the same data set as we used in Chapter 2, but now we trained 100 different networks, varying the number of hidden layer neurons in integer steps from 1 to 100. This will be very tedious if we tried doing so using the nftool like we did in Chapter 2. This is because we will need to repeat that whole procedure for a 100 times. We therefore wrote a MATLAB code that automatically did the training for a 100 times, varying the number of hidden layer neurons in integer steps from 1 to 100. This code is saved as *NNcode.m* in our project folder. For each of the trainings, the code saves the network generated in a folder named *networks* within our project folder. The networks are named net1, net2, net3,…. up to net100, representing the networks obtained in using the number of hidden layer neurons equal to 1, 2, 3,…. up to 100 respectively. In each training, the code also computes the RMSE obtained using the 15% test data (randomly selected) and the RMSE obtained using the year 2016 data. Figure 24 (also produced by the code) illustrates how the RMSEs vary with the number of hidden layer neurons.

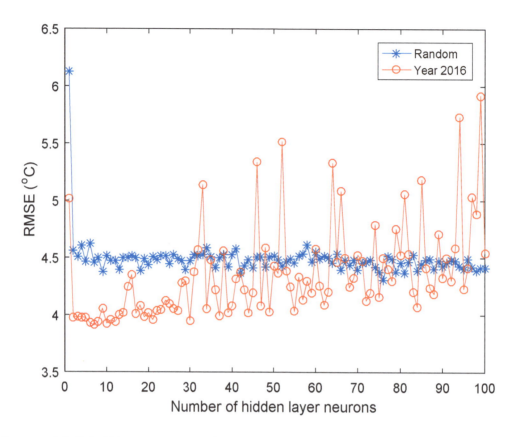

Figure 24. RMSE versus number of hidden layer neurons.

As expected, and as explained earlier, the RMSEs for the 15% random test data show a continuous general decrease with increasing number of hidden layer neurons. This is because these data fall within the range of data used for the training (1965 – 2015). However for the year 2016 test data, the RMSEs started increasing when the number of hidden layer neurons exceeded about 30. The increase shows that, beyond that number, the network predictions were no longer as good as before it. This is because the networks were over-trained when the number of hidden layers exceeded 30; the RMSEs for the random test data kept decreasing (an indication of good predictions), but the RMSEs for the year 2016 test data were now on the increase (indicating bad predictions for the dataset outside the training range).

Going by Figure 24, it is recommended not to use the networks with more than 30 hidden layer neurons. We could regard 30 as the threshold for the number of hidden layer neurons, beyond which the networks over-fit (This boundary is, however, not usually distinct, but it is just an approximation). An optimal network will therefore be that which gave the least RMSE on the year 2016 data, and which does not have more than 30 hidden layer neurons. This is the network with 7 hidden layer neurons (that is the network named *net7* in our *networks* folder).

How did we decide that net7 is the optimal network? There is a file named *rmse.txt* created by the same code that created the networks. This file contains the RMSEs obtained when each of the networks predicts the temperatures for the test data. Figure 25 illustrates the contents of this file.

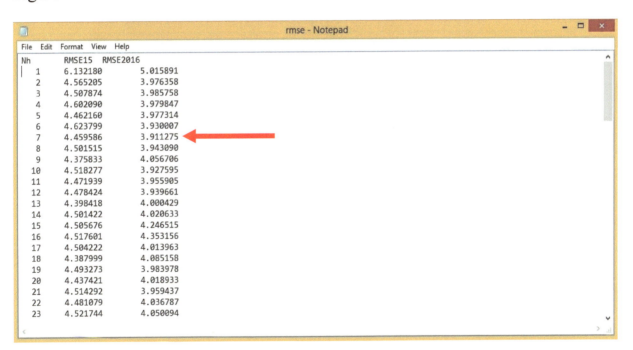

Figure 25. RMSEs for networks of different number of hidden layer neurons

The first column of the file represents the number of neurons in the hidden layer, the second column represents the RMSEs obtained using the 15% test data, and the third column represents the RMSEs obtained using year 2016 data. The file shows that the least RMSE for the year 2016 data is 3.911275, which is the RMSE associated with 7 hidden layer neurons. And that is exactly how we decide an optimal number of hidden layer neuron for the neural network.

Now, we are going to take a similar but extended project. This is for the next chapter.

Chapter 4

Project 2: Time series modeling of instantaneous temperatures

In this project, our interest is to model the temperature at any desired time of the day. The difference between this project and the previous one is that in the previous project, we modeled just the maximum daily temperatures, so we had only one temperature value for a day. In this project, we will be modeling the temperatures for all times of the day, so we could have as much temperatures as possible in a day.

Since we had given a full illustration of processes in the previous project, we will concentrate here on highlighting the advances of this project over the previous one, and explaining how they can be implemented.

For illustration purpose, we will be using temperature data that has been recorded at four different locations in Nigeria. The locations are Abuja (Latitude 9.07° N, Longitude 7.48° E, Altitude 536m), Anyigba (Latitude 7.29°N, Longitude 7.63°E, Altitude186m), Jos (Latitude 9.93°N, Longitude 8.88°E, Altitude981m), and Makurdi (Latitude 7.73°N, Longitude 8.54°E, Altitude140m). The temperature data are obtained from automatic weather stations in the Tropospheric Data

Acquisition Network (TRODAN). The facilities are maintained and operated by the Centre for Atmospheric Research, National Space Research and Development Agency, Anyigba, Nigeria.

The project and the results have been fully described in a research paper; Okoh et al. (2015) published in Weather journal. Here, we shall concentrate in highlighting procedures that will enable readers to successfully perform similar work, and to apply their understandings to designing other projects of their interest. Here we go!

First, we need to understand that the structure of the neural network here will be different from the previous one. How? Since we are interested in creating a model that can give us the temperatures at any desired time of a day, we need an additional input neuron; that is, the Hour of the day. The network here additionally needs to learn the temperature variation patterns over the days. So, the data we need for the training should say the temperatures at particular times of the day.

The data used here was obtained on a 5-minute interval, but to reduce the data and to smoothen the data profiles, we averaged it on an hourly interval, so that we had 24 data points for each day. A pattern of the input data file is illustrated in Figure 26.

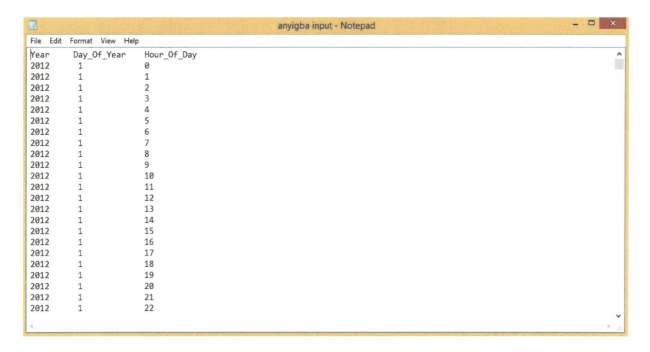

Figure 26. Sample Input Data for Project 2.

The main difference is that, in this project, we have included a third column (representing the Hour of the day). It is this third column that enables the network to learn how the temperatures vary over the hours in a day. We therefore have 3 input layer neurons in this project, as against the 2 we had in the previous project.

We are interested in learning (and predicting) only the temperatures for each set of the 3 inputs, so we have just 1 output layer neuron like in the previous project. The output file should look similar to that of the previous project (having just one column, which represents the temperatures corresponding to data in the input file). Remember that the number of rows in the input file should be the same as in the output file, so that each set of inputs match with an output value.

Every other thing about the training procedure is the same as for the previous project. We did these same procedures for all the four locations, and using similar method described in chapter 3, we obtained optimal values for the number of hidden layer neurons as 12, 13, 15 and 26 for the Abuja, Anyigba, Jos and Makurdi locations respectively. It is important to emphasize, at this stage, that we will not always get these same values even on the same set of training data. This is because neural network trainings progress differently, unlike the case with guided computer programs where we expect to get exactly the same results each time we run a program on the same dataset.

Another major difference between this project and the previous one is that, after the training, we will always require a set of 3 inputs to get an output from the network. The inputs are: Year, Day of year, and Hour of Day. In the previous project, we required only the first two inputs. This is obviously because the network was trained with that set of inputs. To make predictions, neural networks require exactly the same set of input parameters used for their trainings.

Chapter 5

Project 3: Modeling of the Ionospheric TEC over Nigeria using GNSS Data

Just for the sake of persons that may have no knowledge at all of what TEC is, we present a very brief and modest explanation in this paragraph. Total Electron Content (TEC) is a parameter of the ionosphere that gives an overall description of it. The ionosphere is a portion of the upper part of our atmosphere where radiation from the Sun is intense enough to reasonably ionize the atmospheric molecules. As a result of radio signal transmissions from satellites in the Global Navigation Satellite System (GNSS) through the ionosphere down to receivers on Earth, the GNSS provides a wealth of information about the ionospheric TEC. Just like temperature, TEC changes over space and time.

In this project, we will use TEC information obtained from 14 GNSS receivers located in different parts of the country (from years 2011 to 2015). This project has been completely described in the research paper, Okoh et al. (2016). Like in Project 2, our interest here is to highlight advances on this project, so that the reader can understand and implement them even without consulting the mentioned research paper.

First, we mention that, just like in Project 2, we are interested in obtaining the TEC at any time of a day, so we require the same 3 input neurons (Year, Day of year, and Hour of day) as time series indicators.

Next, we explain that one advancement on this project is that we want to model the parameter over the space of the entire country. That is, we additionally want to be able to predict the value at any location in the country, not just at the 14 locations from which we obtained the data. Observe that this is the first project we are doing such. In Project 2, we did use data from 4 different locations, but we trained the data, station by station, and so we got 4 networks, each predicting the temperatures at the 4 different locations. The scenario in this project is different; we are having data from 14 locations, and we are using all of these data to train a single network which will be used to predict the TEC at any location in the country, not necessarily the 14 locations. The network, in this project, will therefore additionally have to learn how the parameter changes over space.

To achieve the spatial training, we need to additionally introduce inputs that indicate locations; the longitudes and latitudes of the locations are perfect for this purpose, and they are what we have used. Just to mention, we used geomagnetic longitudes and latitudes rather than the geographic longitudes and latitudes since they are better pointers of the spatial variations of TEC in the equatorial region (this is the region where Nigeria is). So, we are introducing 2 additional input neurons (the Geomagnetic Longitude and the Geomagnetic Latitude) making a total of 5.

Another advancement on this project is that we have introduced more input neurons. These are parameters that have been known to cause variations in TEC. One of these parameters is the sunspot number (an indicator of solar activeness). Over the years, ionospheric scientists have found that TEC values are usually higher for years of higher solar activity, and vice versa. So, we introduced the sunspot number as an additional input neuron to enable the network to learn variations that are associated with solar activity. This brings the number of input layer neurons in this project to 6.

Next is the introduction of another input neuron; the disturbance storm time (DST) index. The DST index is an indicator of geomagnetic storm activity. Ionospheric scientists have also found that geomagnetic storms cause certain variations in TEC. We introduced the DST as an additional input neuron so that the network can, through it, learn the variations that are associated with geomagnetic storms. This brings our number of input neurons to 7.

Finally, as a novel concept in the work, we introduced one more input neuron (the critical ionospheric plasma frequency, denoted $foF2$). Detailed explanation for the idea behind this inclusion is contained in Okoh et al. (2016), but we highlight here that the $foF2$ is a basic parameter often required as a base for TEC modelling. As demonstrated in the results of Okoh et al. (2016), introduction of the $foF2$ as an input neuron showed huge positive impact on the performance of the network. This brings the number of input neurons to 8, and this is the total number of input neurons used in this project.

We emphasize at this stage that more input neurons can be added to a neural network project, these input neurons should be effective (that is, they should have links with the parameter to be modeled). Effective input neurons usually improve the performance of neural networks. Non-effective ones, on the other hand, are usually setbacks to the neural network performance. This is the aspect where the trainer's knowledge of parameters that affect the parameter to be modeled is required. The trainer should spend some time to think of, and to understand what parameters affect the parameter to be modeled.

As a summary, the required input file for the neural network training in this project should look like in Figure 27. As in the previous 2 projects, the target file should have one column of data representing the TEC values for inputs in the input file. As usual, the number of rows in the target file should be the same as the number of rows in the input file.

NNN1 - Notepad

File Edit Format View Help

Year	DOY	Hour	GeomLatitude	GeomLongitude	foF2	DST	SSN
2011	1	0.00	-0.380000	82.020000	5.410563	-11	48
2011	1	0.50	-0.380000	82.020000	5.236349	-11	48
2011	1	1.00	-0.380000	82.020000	4.991929	-11	48
2011	1	1.50	-0.380000	82.020000	4.640286	-11	48
2011	1	2.00	-0.380000	82.020000	4.183300	-9	48
2011	1	2.50	-0.380000	82.020000	3.658838	-9	48
2011	1	3.00	-0.380000	82.020000	3.162278	-5	48
2011	1	3.50	-0.380000	82.020000	2.819860	-5	48
2011	1	4.00	-0.380000	82.020000	2.740085	-3	48
2011	1	4.50	-0.380000	82.020000	2.991925	-3	48
2011	1	5.00	-0.380000	82.020000	3.546921	-4	48
2011	1	5.50	-0.380000	82.020000	4.353345	-4	48
2011	1	6.00	-0.380000	82.020000	5.282350	-5	48
2011	1	6.50	-0.380000	82.020000	6.195732	-5	48
2011	1	7.00	-0.380000	82.020000	6.973452	-6	48
2011	1	7.50	-0.380000	82.020000	7.556241	-6	48
2011	1	8.00	-0.380000	82.020000	7.915888	-5	48
2011	1	8.50	-0.380000	82.020000	8.077248	-5	48
2011	1	9.00	-0.380000	82.020000	8.092211	-7	48
2011	1	9.50	-0.380000	82.020000	8.012088	-7	48
2011	1	10.00	-0.380000	82.020000	7.895487	-7	48
2011	1	10.50	-0.380000	82.020000	7.782321	-7	48
2011	1	11.00	-0.380000	82.020000	7.698974	-9	48

Figure 27. Sample Input Data for Project 3.

Column 1 of the input data is Year, column 2 is Day of year, column 3 is Hour of day, column 4 is Geomagnetic latitude, column 5 is Geomagnetic longitude, column 6 is *fo*F2, column 7 is DST, and column 8 is Sunspot number.

The training procedure is exactly as with project 1. Using a similar method as described in chapter 3, we obtained 11 as the number of hidden layer neurons for the optimal network.

The final point to note is that, after the training in this project, we will always require a set of 8 inputs to get an output from the network. These are the same 8 input parameters used for the training.

As an illustration, to make a prediction of the TEC for 13:00UT of 4th February 2018, we should create the input as follows:

input = [2018 35 13 a b c d e];

where a and b are respectively the geomagnetic latitude and geomagnetic longitude of the location for which we are making the prediction, c is the *fo*F2 value for the location at time 13:00UT of 4th February 2018, d is the DST index at that time, and e is the sunspot number for the day. Sections 2.5 and 2.6 contain details and the complete codes required to make the predictions. These codes do not change, only the inputs do.

That is it for getting started with neural networks on MATLAB!

References

Baboo SS, Shereef KI. 2010. An efficient weather forecasting system using artificial neural network. Int. J. Environ. Sci. Dev. 1(4): 321–326

Demuth H, Beale M. 2002. Neural Network Toolbox for use with MATLAB. The Mathworks Inc.: Natick, MA.

Kisi O, Uncuoglu E. 2005. Comparison of three back-propagation training algorithms for two case studies. Indian J. Eng. Mater. Sci. 12: 434–442.

Okoh D, Yusuf N, Adedoja O, Musa I, Rabiu B. 2015. Preliminary results of temperature modelling in Nigeria using neural networks, Weather, 70(12): 336-343.

Okoh D, Owolabi O, Ekechukwu C, Folarin O, Arhiwo G, Agbo J, Bolaji S, Rabiu B. 2016. A regional GNSS-VTEC Model over Nigeria using Neural Networks: a novel approach. Geodesy and Geodynamics. 7(1): 19-31.